Olympiad Planner 1

for

(MATHEMATICS, SCIENCE AND ENGLISH OLYMPIADS)

Editorial Board

V&S PUBLISHERS

Published by:

V&S PUBLISHERS
F-2/16, Ansari road, Daryaganj, New Delhi-110002
☎ 23240026, 23240027 • *Fax:* 011-23240028
Email: info@vspublishers.com • *Website:* www.vspublishers.com

Regional Office : Hyderabad
5-1-707/1, Brij Bhawan (Beside Central Bank of India Lane)
Bank Street, Koti, Hyderabad - 500 095
☎ 040-24737290
E-mail: vspublishershyd@gmail.com

Branch Office : Mumbai
Jaywant Industrial Estate, 2nd Floor–222, Tardeo Road
Opposite Sobo Central Mall, Mumbai – 400 034
☎ 022-23510736
E-mail: vspublishersmum@gmail.com

Follow us on:

All books available at **www.vspublishers.com**

ISBN 978-93-579408-8-7
1st Edition

Printed at : Param Offseters Okhla New Delhi-110020

Publisher's Note

V&S Publishers, after the grand success of a number of Academic and General books, is pleased to bring out Olympiad Planners for classes from 1st to 10th under The Gen X series – generating Xcellence in generation X – which helps students to prepare for the Olympiad exams. The planner provides step-wise guidance to go through the exam i.e. *how to register, tips and study chart for efficient preparation, pattern and syllabus of exam, recommended study material and scholarships*. One model paper on Mathematics, Science, Cyber and English Olympiad each has been included for practice purpose.

All planners have been developed to provide systematic guidance to the students who aspire to become Olympiad champs at national and international levels. To get success in Olympiads, students need to do thorough study of topics covered in Olympiad syllabus and the topics covered in school syllabus as well. The tips and tricks given in this planner help candidates to prepare for the exam efficiently. Olympiads check efficiency of candidates in problem solving. These exams are conducted in different stages at regional, national, and international levels. At each stage of the exam, a candidate should be fully prepared to take new challenges. Thus, this exam requires careful attention towards comprehension of concepts and thorough practice.

We wish you all success in the examination and a very bright future.

All the best

Contents

1 Introduction to Olympiads

International Mathematical Olympiad (IMO)

International Mathematical Olympiad (IMO) is a world championship mathematics competition for students of High School and it is held annually in different countries. The first IMO with seven participating countries was held in 1959 in Romania. The scope of this exam was gradually expanded to over 100 countries within five continents. The IMO Advisory Board ensures that the competition takes place every year and that each host country observes regulations and traditions of the IMO.

In India, Mathematics Olympiad is conducted by **Homi Bhabha Centre for Science Education (HBCSE)** which organises this exam on behalf of **National Board for Higher Mathematics (NBHM)** of the Department of Atomic Energy (DAE). **Central Board of Secondary Education (CBSE)** also conducts Group Mathematical Olympiad based on which successful candidates are sent to the International Mathematical Olympiad. A maximum of 30 students from CBSE group are selected (strictly in order of merit) to participate in Indian National Mathematical Olympiad (INMO) conducted by National Board of Higher Mathematics (NBHM). The selection at national level leads to participation at International Mathematical Olympiad. **Science Olympiad Foundation (SOF)** which identifies and encourages mathematical creativity of children also conducts Mathematics Olympiad in schools across India and abroad.

The students from classes 1–12 are eligible to appear in Maths Olympiad. For classes 1–4, 10 questions from Section–1 (Logical Reasoning), 10 questions from Section–2 (Mathematical Reasoning), 10 questions from Section–3 (Everyday Mathematics) and 5 questions from Section–4 (Achievers section) are asked. Thus, the students are required to answer 35 questions in 60 minutes.

For classes 5–12, 15 questions from Section–1 (Logical Reasoning), 20 questions from Section–2 (Mathematical Reasoning), 10 questions from Section–3 (Everyday Mathematics) and 5 questions from Section–4 (Achievers section) are asked. Thus, the students are required to answer 50 questions in 60 minutes.

National Science Olympiad (NSO)

The National Science Olympiad (NSO) is a science competition in Asia. It is conducted in two levels. The students from classes 1–12 are eligible to appear in it. For classes 1– 4, 5 questions from Section–1 (Logical Reasoning) and 25 questions from Section–2 (Science) and 5 questions from Section–3 (Achievers section) are asked in the exam. Thus, the students are required to answer 35 questions in 60 minutes. For classes 5–10, 10 questions from Section–1 (Logical Reasoning) and 35 questions from Section–2 (Science) and 5 questions from Section–3 (Achievers section) are asked. Thus, the students are required to answer 50 questions in 60 minutes. The questions are of Multiple Choice Questions (MCQs) type and students are required to mark their responses on OMR answer sheets.

All the students participating in NSO (1st level) get a Student Performance Report (SPR), with their Score, School Rank, City Rank, State Rank, International Rank and Percentile, as well as a Certificate of Participation. SOF also generates a performance report for all participating schools, known as School Performance Report (SCPR). On the basis of 1st level exam, Gold, Silver and Bronze medals are awarded to 1st, 2nd and 3rd rank holder (with minimum 10 enrolments in the concerned class) and Gold medal to every class topper (if 5–9 students have enrolled) in each participating school. Selected students appear for 2nd level examination and according to 2nd level ranks, the prizes are given. The criteria for selection to 2nd level are as follows: the student should have secured International Rank from 1–500 (both inclusive) and/or State Rank from 1–10 (both inclusive) and/or Student should secure 1st, 2nd or 3rd rank (minimum ten enrollments) and/or a minimum of 30% of total marks. All students participating in NSO (2nd level) are also given a Certificate of Merit. The respective school of each student with International Rank from 1–3 (both inclusive) is awarded a Science Intellect Trophy (SIT) for having the winning students on their rolls.

Thus, Olympiad is a platform that identifies young geniuses and provides them with a unique competitive platform where they can prove themselves.

International English Olympiad (IEO)

International English Olympiad (IEO) is an examination of the first of its kind in the history of English language testing in India. The IEO is a joint venture of the Science Olympiad Foundation and The English and Foreign Languages University (EFLU), Hyderabad. The examination has been developed by a group of professionals who constitute the All India English Language Testing Authority (AIELTA) at The English and Foreign Languages University (EFLU).

The students from classes 1–12 are eligible to appear in International English Olympiad. For classes 1–4, 30 MCQs from Sections 1–3 (Word and Structure Knowledge, Reading, Spoken and Written Expression) and 5 MCQs from Section–4 (Achievers section) are asked whereas for classes 5–12, 45 MCQs are asked from Sections 1–3 (Word and Structure Knowledge, Reading and Spoken and Written Expression) and 5 MCQs from Section–4 (Achievers section) are asked.

2 How to Apply

Registration: The IMO is open to students from 1st to 12th standard. The prospectus containing the registration forms is sent to all the schools which are registered with SOF. The schools which are not registered may also request for prospectus by sending an e-mail at *info@sofworld.org* or by making a phone call to SOF.

Registration of New Schools: The schools which want to participate in the Olympiad are required to send their complete address in the following format.

- School Name : ____________________
- Address : ____________________
- City : ____________________
- State : ____________________
- Pin code : ____________________
- Phone No. with STD Code : ____________________
- E-mail : ____________________
- Principal's Name : ____________________

The SOF will send relevant information and registration forms to the school at appropriate time. The registration forms duly filled in and complete in all respects must be submitted to the SOF by the due date. Last date of receipt of registrations is 30 days before the chosen date of exam.

Roll Numbers: The school's coordinator (teacher) generates students' Roll Numbers as per the guidelines. A copy of these roll numbers along with the Students' Registration Sheet (SRS) and School Registration Form (SRF) should be sent to the Foundation's office on/before the due date of submission of forms. The Foundation will register the applicant school and the students and will dispatch question papers and guidelines for conducting the examination.

Note: Principals/teachers of all participating schools may please note that any school can be registered as a centre for IMO. No fee is required from the institution to be a registered examination centre. For a school to become the centre, at least 10 students need to be registered from the school for feasibility reasons. The IMO is conducted in two days for Level 1. Every school may select a date for conducting the IMO exam as per its convenience. A different question paper will be provided to the students on each day.

The students should register through their respective schools only. An individual registration by students is not acceptable.

Fee Structure

For schools in India: A nominal fee is charged from each student. The school shall retain a part of it per student per Olympiad for its expenses as exam centre. The details about fee/mode of payment etc. are given in detail in Registration Forms sent to the schools.

Mode of Payment: The school can make payment via Demand Draft or through NEFT/ RTGS

- **Demand Draft:** It should be made in favour of **Science Olympiad Foundation** payable at **New Delhi.**
- **NEFT/ RTGS:** Details for NEFT/RTGS are:
  - Beneficiary Name : Science Olympiad Foundation
  - Beneficiary A/C No. : SOFXXXXXX (XXXXXX denotes school Code allotted by Science Olympiad Foundation)
  - Beneficiary Bank Name : ICICI Bank
  - Beneficiary Branch : CMS
  - IFSC Code : ICIC0000103

Schedule of Examination

The schools may select a date for conducting the Olympiads in their school premises. The change in date is not permitted. There are separate question papers for different dates. The participating schools may send registrations latest by 31st August every year.

For knowing the date and schedule of exam, students are advised to contact the co-ordinator of their school.

OR

Visit www.sofworld.org for updates on dates, schedule, and pattern of exam etc.

The schedule of Olympiad exams for 2015-16 is as follows:

1st Level Exams:

EXAM NAME	DATE 1	DATE 2
15th NCO	23rd Sept 2015	8th Oct 2015
18th NSO	20th Oct 2015	5th Nov 2015
9th IMO	26th Nov 2015	10th Dec 2015
6th IEO	20th Jan 2016	28th Jan 2016

2nd Level Exams:

2nd level exam was held on 2nd/ 3rd Sunday of Feb 2016. The 2nd level exam is held for students from classes 3rd to 12th for NCO, NSO and IMO. IEO is a single level exam.

3 Selection Procedure

Selection Procedure for IMO

The selection of student would be done on the basis of performance in the exam. Results of both levels of IMO are declared within 6 weeks of the examination.

- The results are sent to the concerned schools.
- The results are also made available on SOF's website.

International Mathematics Olympiad is conducted in 2 Levels/phases.

Level 1: The first level of the test is organized in the respective schools of the participants during school hours.

(i) The level 1 competition is a written objective type test of 60 minutes' duration comprising 35 objective-type (Multiple Choice) questions for class 2 to class 4 and 50 objective-type (Multiple Choice) questions for class 5 to class 12.

(ii) The question paper consists of:

(a) Logical Reasoning (b) Mathematical Reasoning (c) Everyday Mathematics (d) Achievers Section

(iii) There are separate question papers for each class.

(iv) The medium of the test is English.

(v) CBSE, ICSE/ISC and State Board syllabus is followed for setting the test papers.

(vi) The exam is conducted during school hours.

Level 2: The qualifiers to second round include the following:

(i) Top 5% of candidates class-wise, who appear for the 1st level exam. Due weight-age to marks scored in different sections will be given. Each section is accorded with separate weight-age.

(ii) State-wise top 10 rank holders class-wise.

(iii) Class topper where at least 10 students from a class appear in the exam and scores 75% qualifying marks.

Selection Procedure for NSO

Level 1: The first level of the test is organized in respective schools of participants during school hours.

(i) The level 1 competition is a written objective type test of 60 minutes duration comprising 35 objective type (Multiple Choice) questions for class 2 to class 4 and 50 objective type (Multiple Choice) questions for class 5 to class 12.

(ii) The question paper for class 1st to class 10th consists of:

(a) Logical Reasoning (b) Science (c) Achievers section

(iii) There are separate question papers for each class.

(iv) The medium of the test is English.

(v) CBSE, ICSE/ISC and State Board syllabus is followed for setting test papers.

(vi) The exam is conducted during school hours.

Level 2: The qualifiers to second round would include the following:

(i) Top 5% of candidates class-wise, who appear for the 1st level exam. Due weight-age to marks scored in different sections will be given. Each section is accorded with separate weight-age.

(ii) State-wise top 10 rank holders class-wise.

(iii) Class topper where at least 10 students from a class appear in the exam scores 75% qualifying marks.

Selection Procedure for IEO

Criteria for ranking in 2nd level Olympiad exams:

In case of 2nd level exams, ranks will be accorded on the basis of following criteria:

(i) Total Marks scored in 2nd level exam

In case of a tie of marks, ranks will be finalized as per following order:

(a) Marks scored in sections of 2nd level exam accord more priority.

(b) Total Marks scored in level 1 exam

(c) Marks scored in sections in level 1 exam accord more priority

(d) Past performance of student

(e) Date of Birth - Younger student gets higher priority

Note: In 2nd level, no two students will be given the same rank.

Criteria for ranking- single level Olympiad exams:

For IEO and class 1 and 2 students appearing in NCO, NSO and/or IMO exams, ranks will be accorded on the following criteria:

(i) Marks obtained in the exam.

In case two or more students score same number of marks, ranks will be determined on the following criteria:

(a) Marks obtained in different sections of the exam. Each section is accorded separate priority.

(b) Student's performance in school during previous year - as mentioned in the OMR. This may be verified at the discretion of SOF. Student not stating past year's performance may not be considered for ranking in case of a tie.

(c) Age of student - with greater preference being given to younger student.

(d) Telephonic or personal Interview may be conducted.

No two students will be given same rank. However, in case two or more students score equally on all parameters defined above, the award may be distributed equally among all winners.

4 Syllabus and Curriculum

IMO Class-1

Section 1: Mathematical Reasoning: Numerals, Number Name and Number Sense (2 digit numbers), Addition, Subtraction, Length, Weight, Time, Money, Geometrical Skills.

Section 2: Logical Reasoning: Patterns, Odd One Out, Series Completion, Analogy, Ranking Test, Spatial Understanding, Problems Based on Figures.

Section 3: Achievers Section: Higher Order Thinking Questions - from the above given Syllabus.

NSO Class-1

Section 1: Logical Reasoning: Spatial Understanding, Grouping, Measuring Units, Analogy, Geometrical Shapes, Patterns, Odd One Out, Ranking Test.

Section 2: Science: Living and Non-living things, Plants, Animals, Human Beings and Their Needs, Good Habits and Safety Rules, Air and Water, Weather and the Sky.

Section 3: Achievers Section: Higher Order Thinking Questions - Syllabus as per Section–2.

IEO Class-1

Section 1: Word and Structure Knowledge: Jumbled Letters, Words: Their Meanings and Opposites, Identify the Word From the Picture, Making a Word, Feminine and Masculine, One and Many, Word Pairs, Odd One Out, Animals : Their Babies, Sounds and Groups, Nouns, Verbs, Articles,

Section 2: Reading Comprehension: Comprehension (Prose and Poetry).

Section 3: Achievers Section: Higher Order Thinking Questions - from the above given Syllabus.

5 Pattern of Exam

International Mathematics Olympiad

SOF LEVEL–1

Class	Section	No. of Questions	Marks Per Question	Total Marks
1 to 4	Logical Reasoning	10	1	10
	Mathematical Reasoning	10	1	10
	Everyday Mathematics	10	1	10
	Achievers	5	2	10
	Grand Total	**35**		**40**
5 to 12	Logical Reasoning	15	1	15
	Mathematical Reasoning	20	1	20
	Everyday Mathematics	10	1	10
	Achievers	5	3	15
	Grand Total	**50**		**60**

SOF LEVEL–2

Class	Section	No. of Questions	Marks Per Question	Total Marks
3 to 4	Mathematics	30	1	30
	Achievers	5	2	10
	Grand Total	**35**		**40**
5 to 12	Mathematics	45	1	45
	Achievers	5	3	15
	Grand Total	**50**		**60**

National Science Olympiad

Class	Section	No. of Questions	Marks/ question	Total Marks
1 to 4	Logical Reasoning	5	1	5
	Science	25	1	25
	Achievers Section	5	2	10
	Grand Total	**35**		**40**
5 to 10	Logical Reasoning	10	1	10
	Science	35	1	35
	Achievers Section	5	3	15
	Grand Total	**50**		**60**
11 and 12	Physics & Chemistry	25	1	25
	Achievers Section	5	3	15
	Mathematics/Biology	20	1	20
	Grand Total	**50**		**60**

International English Olympiad

IEO				
Class	**Section**	**No. of Questions**	**Marks per Question**	**Total Marks**
1 to 4	Word and Structure Knowledge	30	1	30
	Reading			
	Spoken and Written Expression			
	Achievers Section	5	2	10
	Grand Total	**35**		**40**
5 to 12	Word and Structure Knowledge	45	1	45
	Reading			
	Spoken and Written Expression			
	Achievers Section	5	3	15
	Grand Total	**50**		**60**

6 Study Chart for Efficient Preparation

IMO CLASS–1

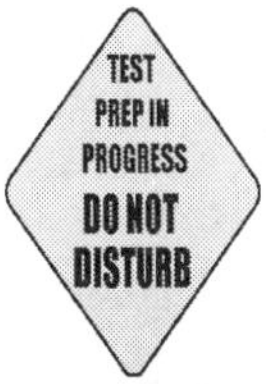	**Week 1** 	**Week 2** 	**Week 3** 	**Week 4** 
Day/Time	**Two Hours**	**Two Hours**	**Two Hours**	**Three Hours**
Monday	Numbers	Geometrical Shapes	Problems Based on Figures	Solved Papers: IMO 2011
Tuesday	Addition	Patterns	High Order Thinking Skills	Solved Papers: IMO 2012
Wednesday	Subtraction	Odd One Out	Revision and High Order Thinking Skills	*Identify your Weak Areas and strengthen the same
Thursday	Measurement	Series Completion	Practice Multiple Choice Question from Section–1	Solved Papers: IMO– 2013
Friday	Time	Analogy	Practice Multiple Choice Question from Section 2	Model Test Paper–1 (Duration: 00 hrs.)
Saturday	Money	Ranking Test	*Identify your weak areas and strengthen the same	*Identify your weak areas and strengthen the same
Sunday	Revision	Revision	Revision	Model Test Paper–2 (Duration: 00 hrs.)

Note:

- Identify your weak areas through detailed reports and strengthen them.
- Practice questions from huge question bank:
  - (i) MTG Workbooks for class 1
  - (ii) 'SOF Olympiad Trainer' Mobile Apps
  - (iii) OSDS (Olympiad Skill Development System)
  - (iv) Olympiads' Books of Reasoning (for preparation of reasoning of Olympiads)
  - (v) E-Quiz
- Take more mock tests to improve your efficiency and become fully prepared for the exam.

NSO CLASS–1

	**Week 1** 	**Week 2** 	**Week 3** 	**Week 4** 
Day/Time	**Two Hours**	**Two Hours**	**Two Hours**	**Two Hours**
Monday	Living and Non-living	Human Beings and Their Needs	Air and Water	Subjective section
Tuesday	Plants	Human Beings and Their Needs	Weather and Sky	Subjective section
Wednesday	Patterns	Analogy	Problems Based on Figures	Achievers Section
Thursday				Revision: Logical Reasoning
Friday	Odd One Out	Ranking Test	Measurement	Model Test Paper–1
Saturday	Animals	Follow Safety Rules	Geometrical Shapes	Model Test Paper–2
Sunday	Self Assessment Test (Duration: 3:00 hrs.)	Self Assessment Test (Duration: 3:00 hrs.)	Self Assessment Test (Duration: 3:00 hrs.)	Previous year NSO Paper

IEO CLASS–1

	WEEK 1 	WEEK 2 	WEEK 3 	WEEK 4 
Day/Time	**Two Hours**	**Two Hours**	**Two Hours**	**Three Hours**
Monday	Jumbled Words	One and Many	Verbs	Rock Band
Tuesday	Words and Their Meanings	Word Pairs	Verbs	Model Test Paper–1
Wednesday	Words and Their Opposites	Odd One Out	Articles	Model Test Paper–2
Thursday	Identifying a Word from the Picture	Animals and Their Young Ones	Articles	Model Test Paper–3
Friday	Making a Word	Nouns	A Ball For My Dog	Model Test Paper–4
Saturday	Feminine and Masculine	Nouns	Buzz, Buzz Bumblebee	Model Test Paper–5
Sunday	Revision	Revision	Revision	Revision

Note:

- Identify your weak areas through detailed reports and strengthen them.
- Practice questions from huge question bank:
  - (i) MTG Workbooks for class–1
  - (ii) 'SOF Olympiad Trainer' Mobile Apps
  - (iii) OSDS (Olympiad Skill Development System)
- Take more mock tests to improve your efficiency and become fully prepared for the exam.

7 Tips to Crack Olympiads

Tips to Crack Maths Olympiad

1. Focus on learning the concepts well and on acquiring the basic skills needed to solve problems.
2. Practise mathematics regularly. Make sure that you are solving as many different types of problems as possible. You can practise lots of questions on different topics from the Internet.
3. Identify the areas of your strength and weakness and focus on weak areas to get better results.
4. Solve model papers and understand the pattern of previous years' papers. This will help you to get acquainted with the pattern and structure of the test.
5. Learn shortcuts to solve various types of questions. Keep these points on your fingertips to save time and work efficiently.
6. Read questions thoroughly. Olympiad problems are known for their complexity, which means you have to take an extra effort.
7. During exam do not waste time in solving difficult questions; rather try some short and easy questions first.
8. Do a lot of practice covering each topic. After that take mock tests, analyse your result, and make an assessment report for your current score.
9. Prepare your notes and important facts to remember and do quick revision before exams. It helps in learning faster.

Tips to Crack Science Olympiad

1. Go through the concepts and ponder about them in a practical way.
2. Learn all the formulae and equations well and prepare notes for quick revision.
3. Do experiments in labs to practice and to learn the concepts well.

4. Learn and remember important shortcuts. They should be on your fingertips. It helps you save time and write answers efficiently.
5. Solve Previous Years Papers and Model Test Papers to understand the pattern and structure of the test.
6. Identify your weak areas and try to focus on the topics to overcome the difficulties.
7. Read every question well before answering. Some problems are typical in nature.
8. Do not waste your time in solving difficult questions. First take up easy questions and solve them.
9. Do quick revision before exams. It also helps in learning faster.

Tips to Crack English Olympiad

1. Read a newspaper every day. It will help you in understanding different types of sentence structures and will enhance your knowledge as well.
2. Go through one page of dictionary daily to enrich your vocabulary. This will add a lot of new words and their meanings in different contexts to your vocabulary.
3. Speak in English with your friends, parents and teachers. It will help you in learning verbal speaking skills.
4. Read grammar books and novels to learn language skills and grasp diverse contexts and themes.
5. Do a lot of practice on verbal and written English exercises daily.
6. Identify the areas of your strength and weakness and focus on weak areas to get better results.
7. Solve model papers and understand the pattern of previous years' papers. This will help you to get acquainted with the pattern and structure of the test.
8. Learn shortcuts to solve various types of questions. Keep these points on your fingertips to save time and work efficiently.
9. Read questions thoroughly. Olympiad problems are known for their complexity, which means you have to take an extra effort.
10. Do not waste time in solving difficult questions; rather try some short and easy questions first.
11. Prepare your notes and important facts to remember and to do quick revision before exams.

General Tips to Crack Olympiad

1. Go through the syllabus before you start preparation for the exam. For SOF Olympiad, you can visit the www.sofworld.org
2. Start preparations at least two months before the due schedule of the exam; go through all the curriculum books and study material.
3. Go through different books; solve questions that are a little tougher than traditional CBSE type questions.
4. Manage time properly. Time management skills can help you go through the exam successfully.
5. Consult your teachers. Approach your teachers and discuss your issues with him/her. He/she would certainly guide you.
6. Don't stress yourself. Take deep breaths, or eat your favourite ice-cream or even go for a long walk with your friend. Do anything that helps you relax before your exams. It is very important to keep your mind calm before any exam.
7. Read a little more text matter than that of your textbooks in order to gain better insight.
8. Just review everything in brief one day before beginning of the Olympiad test.

8 Study Material for Olympiads

Study Material and Coaching for IMO

The following books are recommended for preparation of the Olympiad test:

1. Challenges from the Olympiads by C.R. Pranesachar, S.A. Shirali, B.J. Venkatachala, and C.S. Yogananda
2. Problem Primer for the Olympiad by C.R. Pranesachar, B.J. Venkatachala, and C.S. Yogananda
3. You can also purchase the Olympiad Sample Papers for specific exam from www.classmantra.com. You will get the Practice Test and Mock Test.
4. You can purchase a series of books published by V&S Publishers to get precise study material and practice tests on all Olympiads – Mathematics, Science, Cyber, and English.

If any special coaching or tuition is required to become Olympiad Champion?

Though the series of IMO books published by V&S Publishers containing precise concepts with solved examples, illustrations, and diagrams is sufficient for self preparation, the students who find it difficult to learn on their own should go for special coaching/tuition.

Study Material and Coaching for NSO

The Olympiad resource books published by V&S Publishers for students of classes 1-10 are very useful for learning the concepts and for doing thorough practice. Each book consists of a lot Multiple Choice Questions based on theory, logical and analytical reasoning.

Salient features of each book:

- *Learning milestones* which enlists the topics covered in the chapter.
- *'Did You Know?'* provides extra information related to the chapter.
- *Test Your Skills and Activities* help children to explore their knowledge base.

- *Concept-based questions* are subjective and enhance the writing and learning skills of a student.
- *HOTS* also known as High Order Thinking Skills questions enrich the out-of-the-box thinking of children.
- Each exercise is divided into two sections:
  (i) MCQs based on the chapter and syllabus
  (ii) MCQS given in the Achievers section deal with extreme logics of the given chapter

If any special coaching or tuition is required to become Olympiad Champion?

Though the series of Science Olympiad books published by V&S Publishers, containing precise concepts with solved examples, illustrations, and diagrams is sufficient for self preparation, the students who find it difficult to learn on their own should go for special coaching/tuition.

Study Material and Coaching for IEO

If any special coaching or tuition is required to become Olympiad Champion?

Though the series of English Olympiad books published by V&S Publishers containing precise concepts with solved examples and illustrations are sufficient for self preparation, the students who find it difficult to learn on their own should go for special coaching/tuition.

9 Awards and Scholarships

During the academic year 2014-15, over 31500 schools from more than 1400 cities registered and millions of students appeared for the four Olympiad exams. These Olympiads were conducted across 19 countries. For the academic year 2015-16, the SOF will spend over Rupees ten crores on awards, scholarships, gifts and felicitations etc.

All the aspirants participating in IMO (1st level) get a Math Quotient (MQ), their scores and percentile, ranks at city, state, international levels, as well as a certificate of participation. SOF also prepares a performance report known as School Mathematics Quotient for all the participating schools.

The following awards will be provided to the winners of Olympiads being held during the academic year 2015-16.

Awards for Students/IMO Winners

- **For IMO, NSO, and NCO:** International and State toppers (in 20 zones/states) of classes 3rd to 12th, the awards are given to 2nd level winners.
- **For IEO and winners of IMO, NSO, and NCO class 1st and 2nd:** International and State topper awards will be provided to 1st level winners.
- Each winner will be entitled to one award for an exam. The winners will be entitled to the higher level award only, i.e the international top 3 rank holders will be entitled to awards based on their International ranks. Awards accruing to them for State ranks will be given to the next rank holder. Similarly, school award accruing to a State award winner will be given to the next rank holder.
- All students scoring 100% marks in the 2nd level exams of IMO, NSO, and NCO (1st level exam in IEO) will win special awards consisting of gifts worth Rs.1000/ and Merit Certificates.

Scholarships and Merit Certificates

AT INTERNATIONAL LEVEL		
RANK	SCHOLARSHIP	NO.
1st	Rs.50,000/- each + Gold Medal* + Merit Certificate	47
2nd	Rs.25,000/- each + Silver Medal* + Merit Certificate	47
3rd	Rs.10,000/- each + Bronze Medal* + Merit Certificate	47
AT STATE LEVEL		
RANK	SCHOLARSHIP	NO.
1st	Rs5,000/ - each + Gold Medal* + Merit Certificate	940
2nd	Rs2500/ - each + Silver Medal* + Merit Certificate	940
3rd	Rs1000/ - each + Bronze Medal* + Merit Certificate	940
Rank 4th to 25th	Gifts Worth Rs.1000/- + Merit Certificate	20680

Medals at School Level: 600000 Medals to School Toppers:

- When 10 or more students from one class appear in the exam, *gold, silver and bronze medals are given to top 3 rank holders.
- When 5 to 9 students from a class appear in the exam,* gold medal is given to the top rank holder.

Student Performance Report (SPR)

- Every student who appears in any SOF Olympiad exam is provided with a Student Performance Report (SPR) which is a detailed analysis of how the student attempted in the 1st level Olympiad exam.
- The objective of SPR is to share analysis of performance in the exam with the student and her/his parents. This helps the student knows about the areas of his/her strengths and the areas for improvement on absolute terms and on competitive level consisting of peers from his/her class, who appeared for the Olympiad.

The SPR consists of six sections:

- **Section A:** This section shows the marks obtained by a student and the rank achieved in school/city/state and at international level.
- **Section B:** This section reveals analysis of a student's performance in the Olympiad exams during past 6 years.

- **Section C**: This section consists of a topic-wise performance score of a student.
- **Section D**: This section provides correct answers to the questions asked in the Olympiad exam, the answers given by the student and performance analysis of student's answers with other students at state and international levels.
- **Section E:** This section provides a percentile score analysis of a student in comparison to class, state and international percentiles.
- **Section F:** This section shows analysis of average marks at school, state and international level.
- **Section G**: This section shows topic-wise performance comparison within a state.

Note:

(i) Participation certificate is given to every student.

(ii) Merit certification is given to 2nd level participants.

(iii) Medals are Gold/Silver/Bronze colour plated as applicable.

(iv) Top 25 rank holders from a class and each Olympiad exam will be awarded Gold Medals of Excellence and Merit Certificates of Excellence. This will be applicable for winners from 20 Zones/States for performance in the 1st level Olympiad in NCO, NSO, IMO and IEO.

Special Scholarships

- **Girl Child Scholarship Scheme (GCSS):** Rs.5000/- scholarship to 300 girls each, who are academically brilliant and come from economically weak families.
- **Scholarship for Excellence in English (SEE):** Rs.5000/- scholarship to 120 students each exhibiting excellence in English Language.
- **SOF Academic Excellence Scholarship (AES):** Rs.5000/ scholarship + Trophy to 160 students from class 3rd to class 10th. The student scoring highest number of marks in 3 Olympiad exams during one year/session wins the AES scholarship. The winners are selected from all 20 zones/ states.

Awards for Schools

At International Level		
Category	**Awards**	**No. of Awards**
Best Principal	Rs.25000/- each + Citation + Trophy	10
Best Teacher	Rs.10000/- each + Citation + Trophy	40
At State Level		
Category	**Awards**	**No. of Awards**
Best Principal	Best Principal Rs.10000/- each + Citation + Trophy	100
Best Teacher	Best Teacher Rs.5000/- each + Citation + Trophy	240
At District Level		
Category	**Awards**	**No. of Awards**
Best Principal	Best Principal Rs.2500/- each + Citation + Trophy	300
Best Teacher	Best Teacher Rs.1000/- each + Citation + Trophy	650

School Performance Report (SPR)

- Every school which appears in any SOF Olympiad exam is provided with a School Performance Report (SPR) which is a detailed analysis of how the students in the school individually and in totality performed in the Olympiad exam.
- The objective of the report is to share analysis of performance of the students with the school authority. This helps the schools assess their strength and focus on the topics in which the students are weak in absolute terms and also on a competitive level vis-à-vis other schools.

The SPR consists of four parts:

1. **Part A:** This shows class-wise/student-wise marks and ranks achieved by students at the city, state and international level.

2. **Part B:** This provides topic-wise average school performance and comparison with other schools with standard deviation at school and international level.
3. **Part C:** This includes an average performance comparison of marks scored by students of a school versus marks scored by other students at the state and at international level.
4. **Part D:** This reveals the depth, section-wise comparison of performance of students of a school and students at state and international levels as well.

   Note: Appreciation Mementos to School Principals and Teacher-in-Charge is given also.

10 Model Test Paper (IMO)

Section I: Logical Reasoning

1. How many  are there in the box?

A. 22 B. 23
C. 19 D. 21

2. Complete the given number pattern.

A. 16 B. 15
C. 17 D. 19

3. Number of fishes swim to the left is

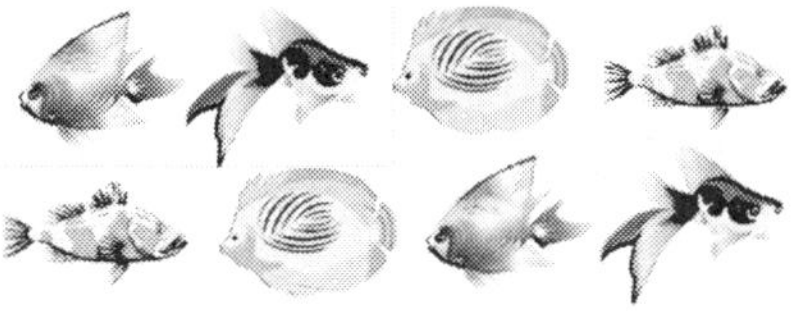

A. 2 B. 3
C. 4 D. 5

4. Minimum number of blocks a mouse run to reach the cake, if it moves only in horizontal and vertical direction, is

A. 9 B. 8
C. 10 D. 7

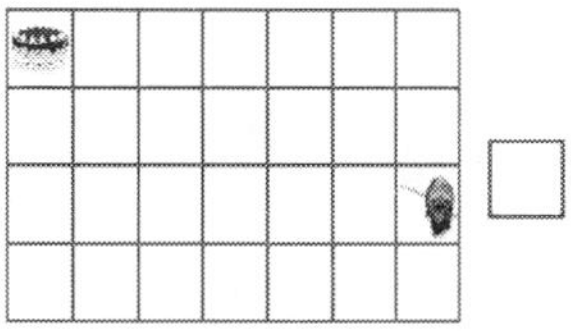

=1 BLOCK

5. Difference between the greatest and smallest number shown on the given butterfly is

A. 87 B. 81

C. 13 D. 80

6. Which of the following shows counting by 5's?

A. 

B. 

C. 

D. 

7. The 7th gift box from the right end is

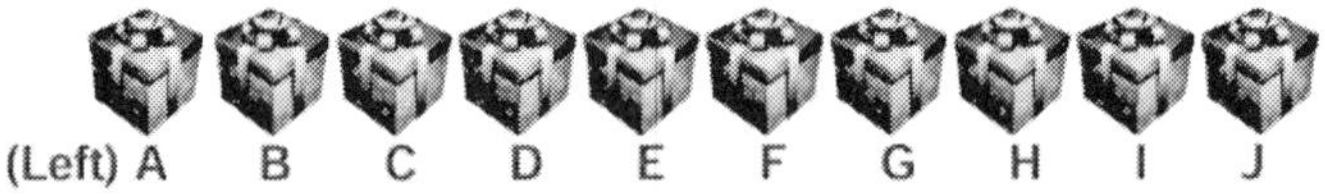

A. D B. C

C. E D. F

8. Number of the groups of 9 paper clips () shown here is

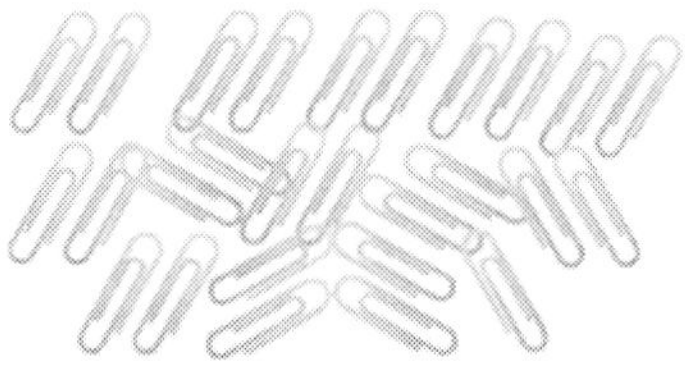

A. 9 B. 27

C. 2 D. 3

9. If 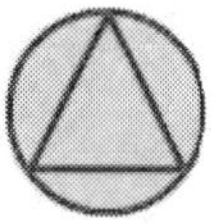 is to 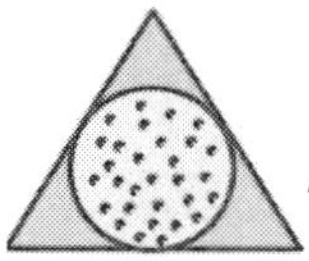, then 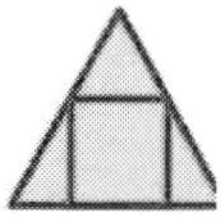 is to

A. 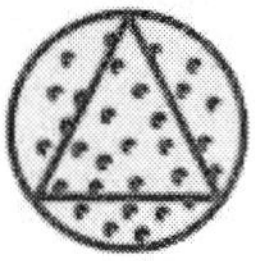

B. 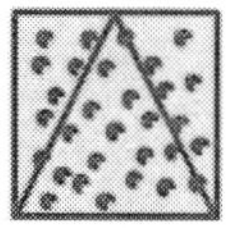

C. 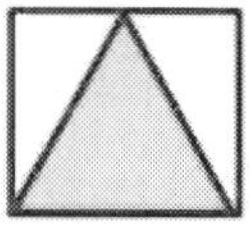

D. 

10. There are ______circles in the given figure.

A. 14
B. 10
C. 13
D. 9

Section II : Mathematical Reasoning

11. Number sentence correctly describing the subtraction shown below is

A. 9 – 4
B. 10 – 4
C. 9 – 5
D. 9 + 4

12. Which abacus shows the total number of balloons given here?

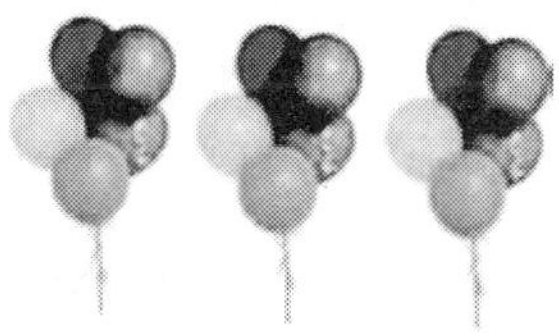

A. 

B. 

C. 

D. 

13. The difference between the number of stones in 6th column and 3rd column is

A. 3
B. 8
C. 7
D. 6

14. Number of Honey comb cells in the given figure is

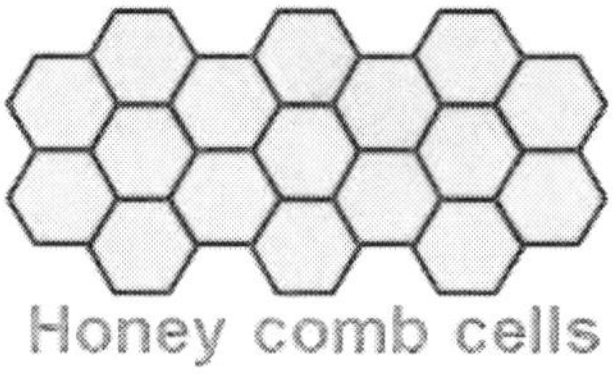

A. 10 ones + 3 ones
B. 10 ones + 2 ones
C. 10 ones + 7 ones
D. 10 ones + 5 ones

15. The given image is how many units tall?

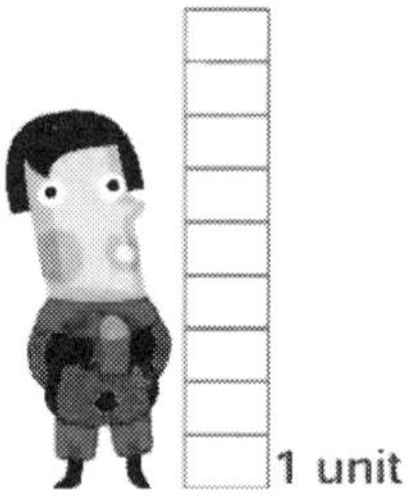

A. 6 units
B. 7 units
C. 5 units
D. 8 units

16. How many given letters are formed ONLY by curved lines?

A B C D E F G H I J K L M N O P Q R S T U V W X Y Z

A. 3
B. 6
C. 5
D. 4

17. There are 8 legs. How many horses are there?

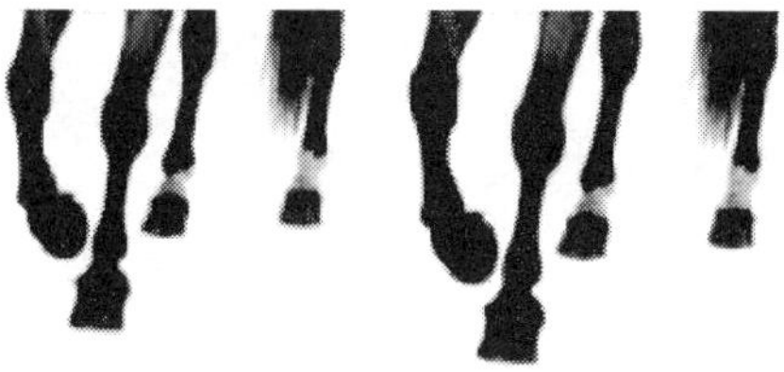

A. 3 B. 4

C. 2 D. 1

18. How many vertical lines are there in the given figure?

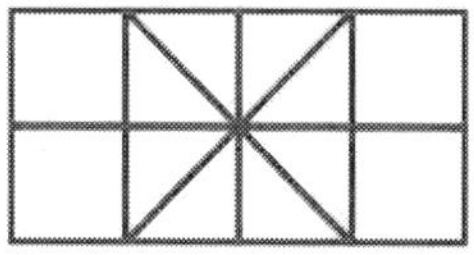

A. 2 B. 4

C. 3 D. 5

19. Kavita has fourteen strawberries. She eats five of them.
Number sentence showing how many strawberries left with Kavita is

A. $14 - 5 = 9$ B. $14 + 5 = 19$

C. $14 - 5 = 8$ D. $14 + 5 = 18$

20. A B C D E F G H I J K L M N O P Q R S T U V W X Y Z

The number of letters lying between which of the following options is the greatest?

A. A and L B. C and M

C. N and W D. Q and Z

21. Which of the following shows descending order?

A. 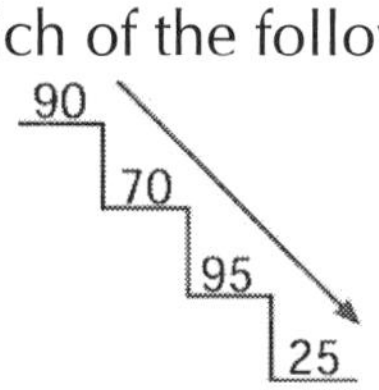

B. 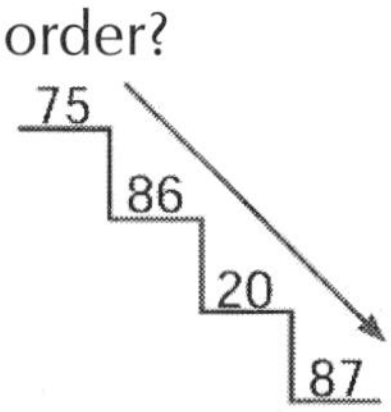

C. 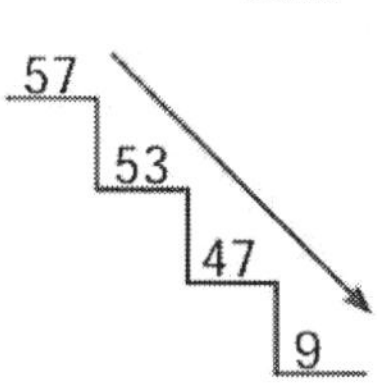

D. 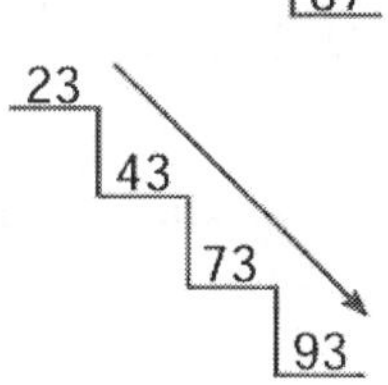

22. How much money is shown here?

A. ₹ 70
B. ₹ 75
C. ₹ 76
D. ₹ 71

23. The difference betwwen third and fifth balloon is

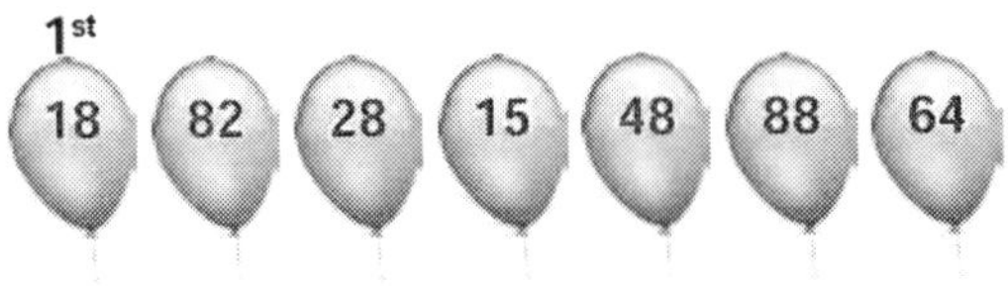

A. 18
B. 30
C. 20
D. 23

24. I am less than 87 but greater than 85. What number am I?

A. 88
B. 86
C. 84
D. 85

25. Which two numbers when added will give 2 tens – 8 ones?

A.

B.

C.

D.

Section III : Everyday Mathematics

26. Latika has 25 stickers. She gives 5 stickers to each of her student. Number of students who will get stickers is

A. 4
B. 6
C. 3
D. 5

27. Total length of Komal's and Beena's pencil is

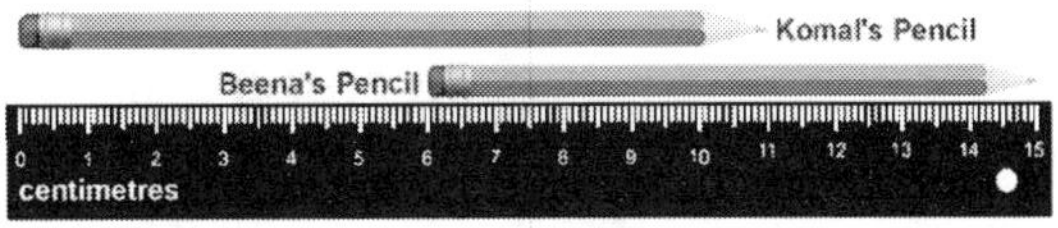

A. 21 centimetres
B. 31 centimetres
C. 17 centimetres
D. 20 centimetres

28. Jiya picked 9 flowers. Ash picked two flowers. Mannu picked 5 flowers. How many flowers did the children pick in total?

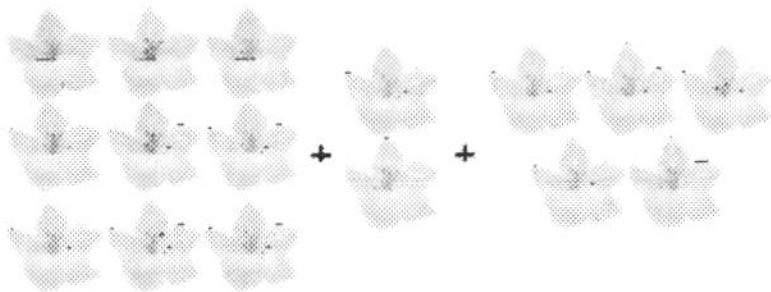

A. 16
B. 14
C. 19
D. 15

29. There are some dogs and cats in the playground. Total number of animals in the playground is

A. 16
B. 19
C. 17
D. 15

30. Out of 35 stamps, Anu gave 13 stamps to NehA. How many stamps does Anu have now?

A. 35
B. 48
C. 22
D. 21

31. A doll costs ₹ 19. Jenny has only ₹ 15 now. How much more money does she need to buy the doll?

A. ₹ 4
B. ₹ 34
C. ₹ 3
D. ₹ 5

32. The given poster of Apu shows different types of fishes. Which type of fish is least in number?

A. 

B. 

C. 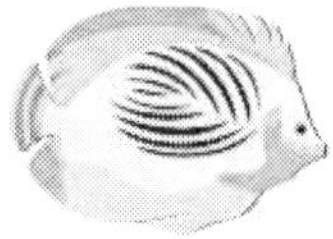

D. 

33. If there are 12 pears altogether and 5 are kept outside, then how many pears are there in the bag?

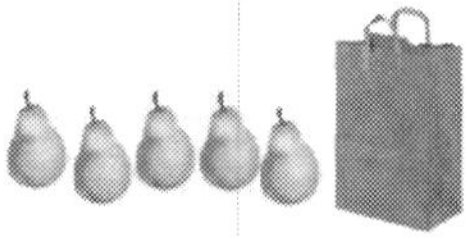

A. 8
B. 6
C. 7
D. 9

34. The total height of both the poles (A and B) together is .

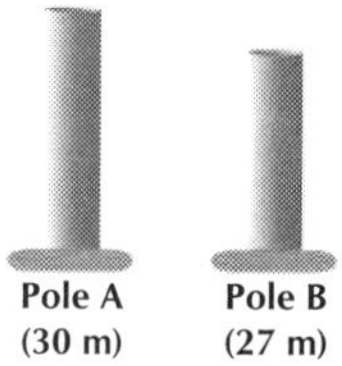

A. 30 metres
B. 57 metres
C. 27 metres
D. 67 metres

35. Which of the following T-shirts bears the number 3 tens + 3 ones?

A. 

B. 

C. 

D. 

11 Model Test Paper (NSO)

1. Look at the pictures given below. Can you identify the creeper?

A. 

B. 

C. 

D. 

2. Which stage of bean germination requires the least sunlight?

A. 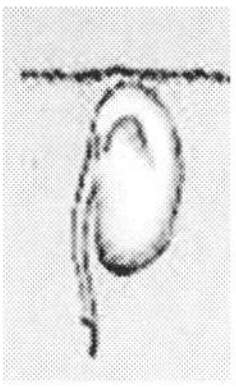

B. 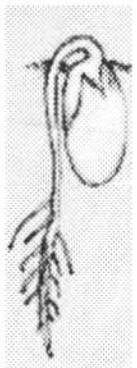

C. 

D. 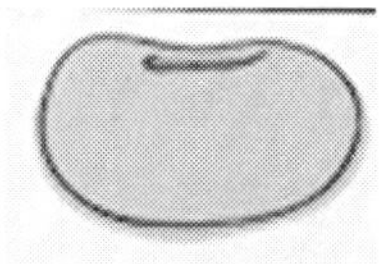

3. Study the following flow chart carefully. Which of the following options can correctly fill the empty box of the flow chart?

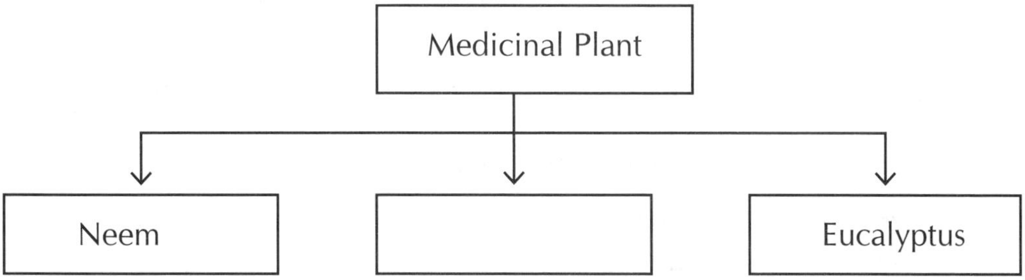

A. Tulsi
B. Maize
C. Sugarcane
D. Cotton

4. How many seeds are present in the following fruit?

A. One
B. Two
C. Four
D. Many

5. Study the given figure. What would X and Y be?

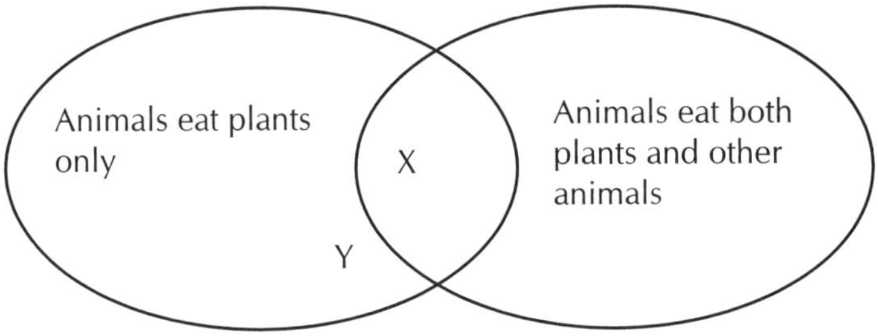

A. X: Bear Y: Squirrel
B. X: Squirrel Y: Cow
C. X: Lizard Y: Bear
D. X: Giraffe Y: Bear

6. Who am I?
   1. I have yellow and brown stripes on my body.
   2. I am the national animal of India.

A. Tiger
B. Lion
C. Cheetah
D. Zebra

7. Choose the correct match:

Animal	Types of food they eat
A. Deer	Plants and animals
B. Hen	Grains
C. Mouse	Flesh of other animals
D. Eagle	Plants

8. This animal lives in:

A. 

B. 

C. 

D. 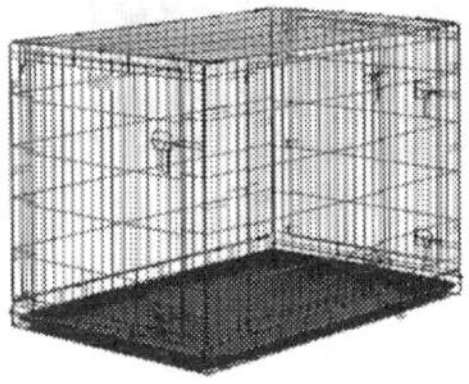

9. Shruti is listening to music. Which sense organ she is using?
   A. Eye
   B. To ague
   C. Skin
   D. Ear

10. This is called a house:

A. 

B. 

C. 

D. All of them

11. Look at the following pictures and mark the foods that help us fight illness and to be healthy.

A. 

B. 

C. 

D. 

12. For healthy muscles, we should eat:
    A. Pulses
    B. Cereals
    C. Fruits
    D. Vegetables

13. Look at the pictures given below.

1. 

2. 

3. 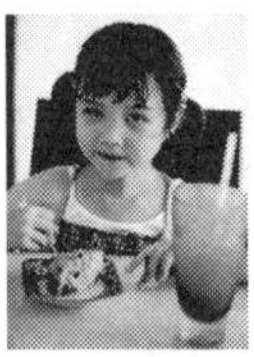

4. 

Which boy/girl is having healthy food?

A. 1 and 4 B. 1 and 3

C. 1 only D. 3 only

14. What is wrong in the following picture?

A. Boy is weak
B. Boy is sitting in a wrong posture
C. A and B both
D. None of the above

15. Look at the given pictures carefully. In which category can we put them?

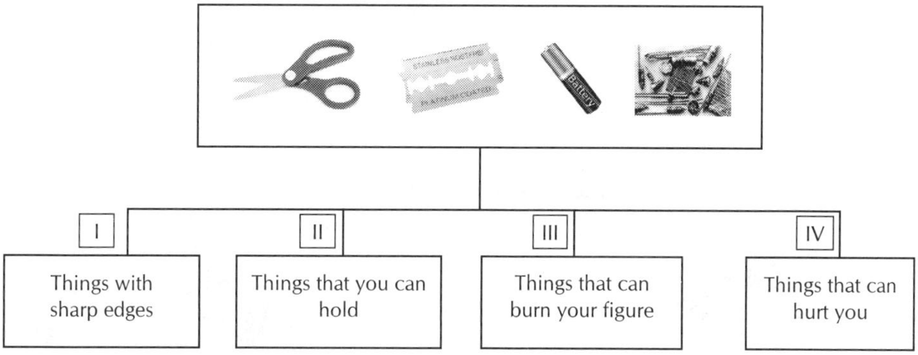

A. I
B. II
C. III
D. IV

16. You should cover your mouth while:

A. 

B. 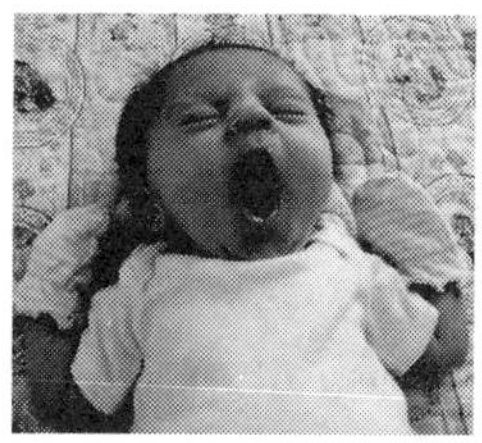

C. 

D. All of these

17. What does the following picture show?

A. Watchman
B. Gate keeper
C. Traffic police
D. Driver

18. Which of the following need air to breathe?

A. 

B. 

C. 

D. A and B both

19. Sanchit wants to play with water. He took a glass, tilted it, and slowly pushed it down into a tub of water. He saw bubbles coming out of the glass.

What does this activity show?

A. Water displaces air in the glass
B. The empty glass is filled with air
C. Air comes out of the water in the form of bubbles
D. All of the above

20. Which of the following is a use of water?

A. We need water to drink
B. People go to water parks to relax and enjoy
C. Water is used for putting out fire
D. All of them

21. Look at the following pictures carefully. The picture shows that:

A. Air occupies space
B. Air has temperature
C. Air has no weight
D. All of the above

22. In which season we see insects and frogs around?

A. Spring B. Rainy
C. Summer D. Winter

23. Look at the following picture.

A. Sunny day B. Rainy day
C. Cold day D. windy day

Among which of these days may see a rainbow in the sky?

24. The sun gives us ______________.

A. Light B. Water
C. Heat D. A and C both

25. Which of the following statements is correct about the moon?

A. The moon gives us light in the day
B. The moon never changes its size
C. The moon is a star
D. The moon is a natural satellite of the Earth

Answer Key

1. C 2. D 3. A 4. D 5. D 6. A 7. B 8. B 9. D
10. B 11. B 12. A 13. A 14. B 15. B 16. D 17. C 18. D
19. B 20. D 21. A 22. B 23. B 24. D 25. D

12 Model Test Paper (IEO)

WORD AND STRUCTURE KNOWLEDGE

1. Find the odd one out from the given sets of words.
   PLANE, TRAIN, BOOK, SHIP, BOAT

   (a) PLANE (b) BOAT (c) BOOK (d) SHIP

2. Identify the picture

   (a) CLOUD (b) BALLOON (c) BUBBLE (d) HOT-AIR BALLOON

Direction (Q. No. 3 and 4) : Identify the object in the picture and fill in the blanks.

3. PENG _ _ N

(a) PENG UI N (b) PENG IU N (c) PENG OI N (d) PENG IO N

4. The young one of a penguin is called ______________.

(a) CALF (b) CHICK (c) NESTLING (d) CYGNET

Direction (Q. No. 5 and 6): Form a meaningful word from the given alphabets and choose the correct option.

5. KCHEC

(a) ECCHK (b) KEHCC (c) CHECK (d) HCECK

6. GHTIL

(a) LIGHT (b) GITHL (c) TIGLH (d) ILGHT

7. Combine the following two words to form a new word:

+

=

SCARE CROW ______________

8. 'Matthew goes to church everyday'. Identify the verb.

(a) Goes (b) Everyday (c) Matthew (d) Church

9. The .... are repairing the broken bridge

(a) man (b) mens (c) men (d) mans

READING

Direction (Q. No. 10 to 13) : For the given picture, answer the following questions.

10. My name is Edward. I am a ________.
   (a) Gardener (b) Teacher (c) Fireman (d) Doctor

11. I am usually found in _______.
   (a) Fire stations (b) Schools (c) Gardens (d) Hospitals

12. I rescue people from __________________.
   (a) Stray dogs (b) Robbers (c) Pests (d) Burning buildings

13. I move around in a ____________.
   (a) Train (b) Fire engine (c) Ship (d) Plane

SPOKEN AND WRITTEN EXPRESSION

Direction (Q. No. 14 and 15) : Choose the right answer.

14. Nelson goes to St. Xavier's High School.

   ....

   (a) There is a big pool next to the house
   (b) The library is far away from the house.
   (c) His school has a big playground.
   (d) The elephant in the zoo is very weak.

15. Mother: Brian, here is your Christmas present.
   Brian: ....
   (a) I don't care. (b) This isn't what I wanted.
   (c) Thank you, Mom. (d) Sorry, I feel asleep.

Answer Key

Word and Structure Knowledge

1.(C) 2. (D) 3. (A) 4. (B) 5. (C) 6. (A) 7. SCARECROW 8. (A) 9. (C)

Reading

10.(C) 11. (A) 12. (D) 13. (B)

Spoken and Written Expression

14. (C) 15. (C)

V&S PUBLISHERS
OLYMPIAD
Planner
1
2
3
4
5
6
7
8
9
10
MATHEMATICS
SCIENCE
ENGLISH
CYBER
The Gen X Series